Life in the Early Islamic World

Trade and Commerce
in the Early Islamic World

Allison Lassieur

Crabtree Publishing Company
www.crabtreebooks.com

Life in the Early Islamic World

Author: Allison Lassieur
Publishing plan research and development:
  Sean Charlebois, Reagan Miller
  Crabtree Publishing Company
Editor-in-Chief: Lionel Bender
Editors: Simon Adams, Lynn Peppas
Proofreaders: Laura Booth, Wendy Scavuzzo
Editorial director: Kathy Middleton
Design and photo research: Ben White
Production: Kim Richardson
Prepress technician: Katherine Berti
Print and production coordinator:
  Katherine Berti
Consultants:
  Barbara Petzen, Education Director,
  Middle East Policy Council and President,
  Middle East Outreach Council;

  Brian Williams, B.A., Educational
  Publishing Consultant and Editor.

Cover: Camel caravan in Sahara desert (center);
  Vintage Ottoman Empire coin (gold coin); Ancient
  Silver Dirham of Baghdad, 786-809AD (silver coin);
  Sailing boat in the Euphrates, from "The Maqamat"
  (The Meetings) by Al-Hariri (bottom right); dried
  spices in a street shop in Marrakesh, Morocco
  (bottom left)
Title page: A market in Egypt

This book was produced for Crabtree Publishing
  Company by Bender Richardson White.

Photographs and reproductions:
The Art Archive: 5 (Bodleian Library Oxford), 9 (Bibliothèque
  Nationale Paris), 10 (Bodleian Library Oxford), 11 (Turkish
  and Islamic Art Museum Istanbul/Gianni Dagli Orti), 12
  and 13 (Topkapi Museum Istanbul/Gianni Dagli Orti),
  17 (Museo Correr Venice/Collection Dagli Orti), 18
  (University Library Istanbul/Gianni Dagli Orti), 22
  (Bargello Museum Florence/Collection Dagli Orti),
  28, 29 (Museo Correr Venice/Collection Dagli Orti),
  35 (Geographical Society Paris/Gianni Dagli Orti),
  40 (Museo Correr Venice/Collection Dagli Orti), 41
  (New York Public Library/Harper Collins Publishers)
The Bridgeman Art Library: Photo © AISA: cover-bottom
  right)
Getty Images: 16, 23 (National Geographic), 24 (Feliks
  Michal Wygrzywalski)
shutterstock.com: cover-center (Galyna Andrushko), cover-
  gold coin (David Mail), cover-silver coin (Kenneth V.
  Pilon), cover-bottom left) (elena moiseeva), 1 (Mirek
  Hejnicki), 3 (JM Travel Photography), 26 (Cardaf), 31
  (Galyna Andrushko), 33 (Attila JANDI), 36 (Valery
  Shanin), 37 (Krzysztof Slusarczyk), 38 (Jan S.). Topfoto
  (The Granger Collection): 6, 8–9, 14, 21, 27, 32, 34, 39, 43;
  30 (Ullsteinbild). Werner Forman Archive: 15 (National
  Maritime Museum, Greenwich), 20 (Statens Historiska
  Museum, Stockholm), 25 (Institute of Oriental Art,
  Chicago).
Maps:
Stefan Chabluk

Library and Archives Canada Cataloguing in Publication

Lassieur, Allison
    Trade and commerce in the early Islamic world / Allison Lassieur.

(Life in the early Islamic world)
Includes index.
Issued also in electronic formats.
ISBN 978-0-7787-2172-7 (bound).--ISBN 978-0-7787-2179-6 (pbk.)

    1. Islamic Empire--Commerce--Juvenile literature. 2. Islamic
Empire--Economic conditions--Juvenile literature. I. Title. I. Series:
Life in the early Islamic world.

HC499.L37 2012   j381.0917'67   C2012-900285-2

Library of Congress Cataloging-in-Publication Data

Lassieur, Allison.
Trade and commerce in the early Islamic world / Allison Lassieur.
    p. cm. -- (Life in the early Islamic world)
Includes index.
  ISBN 978-0-7787-2172-7 (reinforced library binding : alk. paper) --
ISBN 978-0-7787-2179-6 (pbk. : alk. paper) -- ISBN 978-1-4271-9842-6
(electronic pdf) -- ISBN 978-1-4271-9565-4 (electronic html)
  1. Islamic Empire--Commerce--Juvenile literature. 2. Islamic Empire--
Economic conditions--Juvenile literature. I. Title.

HC415.15.L37 2012
381.0956--dc23
                                                    2012000078

Crabtree Publishing Company

www.crabtreebooks.com   1-800-387-7650

Printed in Canada/022012/AV20120110

Published in Canada
Crabtree Publishing
616 Welland Ave.
St. Catharines, Ontario
L2M 5V6

Published in the United States
Crabtree Publishing
PMB 59051
350 Fifth Avenue, 59th Floor
New York, New York 10118

Published in the United Kingdom
Crabtree Publishing
Maritime House
Basin Road North, Hove
BN41 1WR

Published in Australia
Crabtree Publishing
3 Charles Street
Coburg North
VIC, 3058

Contents

About This Book

Islam is the religion of Muslim people. Muslims believe in one God. They believe that the prophet Muhammad is the messenger of God. Islam began in the early 600s C.E. in the Arabian peninsula, in a region that is now the country of Saudi Arabia. From there, it spread across the world. Today, there are about 1.5 billion Muslims. About half of all Muslims live in southern Asia. Many Muslims also live in the Middle East and Africa, with fewer in Europe, North America, and Australia.

Trade and Commerce in the Early Islamic World looks at how Muslim people from around 550 C.E. to 1800 earned their living. It describes and illustrates their work, the products they made, their means of transportation, and their business with other peoples.

In the Beginning

Long before the prophet **Muhammad was born in the city of** Mecca **in 570 C.E., the area where** Islam **would begin was already busy with** trade. Merchants **crossed the region of Arabia buying and selling goods.**

Early Trading Cultures

For centuries, traders had traveled from Europe to the Mediterranean region and traded throughout the Middle East, Asia, and Africa. The **empire** of Greece, and then the Roman Empire had controlled this **commerce**. Their power extended into the lands that are now Saudi Arabia, Syria, Palestine, Egypt, Iran, and Turkey. After the Roman Empire ended in the late 400s, some of the trade routes the Romans had controlled fell out of use. Others were taken over by new and rising empires, such as the Sassanid Empire of Persia (now Iran) and the Byzantine Empire to the west.

Before the rise of Islam, the **Arab** peoples were primarily **nomads**, living in small tribes. The tribes had different religions and ways of life. Each tribe traded with its friends and raided its enemies. Traders traveled across the desert together in small **caravans**, or groups of people, stopping wherever there was water. A few merchants sailed in small ships along the coasts of the Indian Ocean, staying close to land. They traded in iron, steel, horses, incense, and spices. Some traveled to India and even to Southeast Asia, but most trade was local. Most customers wanted everyday items such as food, farm animals, cloth, and tools.

Islamic Timeline

570 Muhammad born in Mecca
610 Muhammad tells people of his first message
622 Muhammad's followers leave Mecca for Medina
630 Muhammad returns to Mecca
632 Muhammad dies
638 **Muslim** armies capture Jerusalem
642 Muslim armies conquer Sasanians
661–750 Umayyad **Caliphate**
750–1258 Abbasid Caliphate
929 Abd al-Rahman III becomes caliph in Córdoba, Spain
1096 First Christian **Crusade** begins
1171–1250 Ayyubid Caliphate
1193 Muslim rule in Delhi, India
1281–1324 Osman I establishes the Ottoman state in Anatolia, Turkey
1453 Ottoman **sultan** Mehmed II finally conquers Byzantine Empire
1632–1653 Taj Mahal built in India
1918 Ottoman Empire ends after Turkey's defeat in World War 1

Muhammad and the religion of Islam united the tribes. After Muhammad's death in 632, Muslims moved far across the Middle East and North Africa. As the Islamic state expanded, Muslims found vast new areas for trade and commerce. Stability created enormous wealth for the new Muslim society, and the Islamic world began its Golden Age.

Below: Islamic markets were busy places. Potters, metalworkers, and other craftspeople produced a wide range of goods for sale. Merchants and traders bought and exchanged these goods.

Above: Inside this covered Turkish **bazaar**, merchants set out their goods as customers enter on horseback.

Muhammad

Muhammad was born into a merchant family. When he was 12, he went on his first trading expedition, to the city of Basra. When he grew up, Muhammad became respected and trusted as a merchant. While earning his living in trade, he had the religious experiences that led him to found Islam.

Mecca—A Great Trading City

Even before the rise of Islam, Mecca was a rich and locally powerful trading city. For an agreed period each year, local tribes living around Mecca stopped fighting so everyone could worship their gods at the *Kaaba*, a shrine, and trade in peace. There, tribes got down to the business of commerce, making deals and exchanging goods with Meccan merchants.

Caravans filled with food, leather, medicines, and animals poured into the city. Some tribes did business with merchants from China and Africa. In this way, spices, silk, and slaves were brought to Mecca's markets. Muhammad was a merchant in Mecca, and it was there that he began to preach the message of Islam. Part of this message criticized the inequality of wealth in the city. When Muhammad took control of Mecca in 630, he made the Kaaba the holiest site in Islam.

Cities of the Middle East

Before the rise of Islam, most trade in the Arab world centered on ports around the eastern Mediterranean and Red seas. Mecca was an important trading city because it was situated on trade routes that linked it to overland routes crossing Arabia, Syria, Iraq, and the Middle East, as well as sea routes in the Red Sea, Mediterranean Sea, and the Persian Gulf.

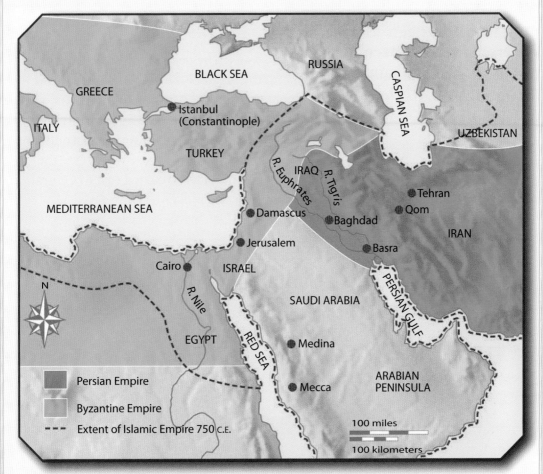

At the time of Muhammad, two empires controlled the Middle East. The Byzantine Empire was based in Constantinople and ruled most of the lands around the Mediterranean Sea. The Sasanians ruled what are now Iran and Iraq from their capital, Ctesiphon. Both empires were later overthrown by Muslim armies.

Growth of Empire

When Muhammad died in 632, he left behind a small community of Muslim believers. Some local tribes turned back to their old religions. Others chose to remain Muslims and had to select new leaders. The leaders of the Muslim community who succeeded Muhammad were called caliphs. Early Islamic states were thus called caliphates.

Below: A caravan of camels makes its way through the snowy Pamir Mountains of Central Asia.

Extending the Empire

The first caliph, Abu Bakr, made war on those Arabs who had turned away from Islam. Within two years, he ruled a single large Islamic state covering the Arabian **peninsula**—land largely surrounded by water. The next caliphs rapidly expanded the reach of the Islamic state beyond Arabia. The Muslims swiftly took over Syria, Palestine, and Egypt from the Byzantines, and Mesopotamia and Iran from the Sasanians. By the 700s, the Islamic state stretched east to Central Asia and India.

Trading Routes

As the Islamic state expanded, trade grew quickly between various peoples in the new empire. Older trade towns, such as Mecca, became busy hubs, or centers, for caravans. They were also hubs for a trade network that stretched from Europe to eastern China.

Sea routes through the Mediterranean Sea and the Indian Ocean became part of the Islamic trade system. These were used in parallel with overland trade routes across Asia to China. Muslim merchants invented ways to help long-distance trade. **Moneychangers** set up banks that made it possible for merchants to borrow and put money away safely even when far from home. They used bills of exchange the way we use checks today. As people of many different religions, languages, and customs traded together, cities became cosmopolitan, which is a mix of cultures.

War and Trade

Muslim leaders considered trade and commerce when they were planning new military campaigns. A successful conquest spread Islam and helped Muslims find new materials, control new trade routes, and open new areas for trade. The Muslim conquest of West Africa, for instance, aimed to take control of the gold, salt, and slave trades—and it succeeded (see pages 22–23 and 34–35).

Right: A map from 1375 shows Italian adventurer Marco Polo and his brothers (right) following Muslim traders (left).

Mapping the World

The Golden Age of the Islamic Empire began in the 900s. It was a time of great achievements, riches, and power. Trade, philosophy, science, medicine, and the arts were at their peak. Old boundaries and tribal divisions were gone because Islam had brought so many societies under one rule. There was peace after many years of war and lawlessness.

As a result, trade throughout the Islamic world was easier, safer, and reached much farther. Muslim merchants set up trading bases as far away as India, Malaya, the East Indies, the Philippines, and China. Trade routes bustled with caravans going back and forth from China to Western Europe and from Russia to Central Africa.

Expanding Trade

Traders moved among the cities of the Abbasid Empire (750–1258), dealing in basic goods people needed. These included grains, and raw materials such as metals and wood. They also traded medicines, paper, and sugar. Rich people wanted luxury goods, too, which had to be imported from far away. To satisfy this demand, traders moved these valuable items from one region to another: pearls from the Persian Gulf, livestock from the Arabian peninsula, frankincense from Yemen, and slaves and ivory from North Africa. All of this trade provided work for craftspeople, metalworkers, bankers, merchants, and shipworkers.

Above: Maps made by Muslim geographers, such as this 1154 map by Abu Abdallah al-Idrisi, are arranged with south at the top. The map shows North Africa and Europe. Al-Idrisi lived and worked in Sicily at the court of the Christian King Roger II.

Trade between Arab peoples and China began before the rise of Islam, but grew during Islam's Golden Age. The most useful invention to come from China was paper. The secret of papermaking spread from China to the Islamic world during the 700s. Paper became an important sales item. Using paper for writing helped Muslim merchants keep good records of their business. Paper was cheap, so it stimulated the production and sale of books in Muslim communities.

Right: As trade moved goods between cultures, artistic ideas moved with them. This incense burner made in the Ottoman Empire in the 1600s combines Chinese **porcelain** in a brass enclosure with Islamic designs.

Trade With the East

Throughout the early Islamic period, trade across Europe, Asia, and Africa was controlled by competing rulers and states. As new trade routes were set up, others were closed because of wars. Asian rulers dominated the Silk Road, the 4,000-mile (6,437-kilometer) network of trails and tracks between the Mediterranean region and China. Merchants, religious teachers, soldiers, explorers, and nomads all traveled the Silk Road in both directions. They took with them not only goods, geographic knowledge, and artistic ideas, but also religions, diseases, and settlers.

Above: This of two Chinese women sitting reading a book was made in Tabriz, Persia. It highlights the mix of ideas and art between different early empires.

Two-Way Traffic

Muslim traders especially valued Chinese goods such as silk and porcelain. Not until the 1700s—more than 1,000 years after the trade began—was the secret of Chinese porcelain known in the West. The Chinese wanted Muslim traders to bring them horses from the Middle East and the metal cobalt from Iran, which they used to make blue-and-white pottery.

Trade Expansion

In 755, the Muslim caliph Abu Jafar-al-Mansur sent thousands of soldiers to help the Chinese emperor, Su Tsung, fight a war. Most of the soldiers were Muslims. After the fighting was over, many of the soldiers stayed in China. They married Chinese women and established Muslim villages and towns.

This Muslim presence in China made it easier for trade to grow between Asia and the Middle East. As the Islamic Empire expanded, Muslim merchants used overland routes and sea routes to trade with China and visit cities in Southeast Asia.

Ports on the coast of the Malayan peninsula, and on the islands of Sumatra and Java, became meeting places for Chinese and Muslim merchants. There they did business and exchanged goods. Muslim merchants arrived with ivory, horses, and gum resins used for incense. The Chinese loaded these goods onto their ships, while the Muslims packed Chinese porcelain and silk for the long journey back westward. Southeast Asian products included sweet-smelling woods from the rainforests and spices such as cloves, nutmeg, and mace. These goods were traded north to China, and west to India, the Middle East, and the Mediterranean lands.

Above: Chinese porcelain was so delicate and expensive that it was always carried with the greatest care. Here it is shown carried in a metal cart pulled by an ass.

Trade With Spain

Islamic armies invaded southern Europe in the early 700s. The Muslims conquered most of Spain and all of Portugal and even invaded southern France. Muslim rulers, known in Europe as **Moors**, ruled in Spain until the 1400s, when the last Moorish king was driven out.

Islamic rule had a great effect on trade and technology. Spain became a major center in the Islamic trade network. Goods from the Islamic Empire and beyond arrived at Spanish ports and were traded on to northern Europe. Traders from the Islamic world brought cloth, incense, spices, foods, ceramics, and other goods to Spain. In return, Spain supplied raw materials, such as timber and iron. There was also a trade in slaves from Spain to the Arabian peninsula.

Above: A Spanish Muslim (left) and a Christian play music together on their citterns, a type of lute. This illustration comes from a Spanish manuscript from the 1200s.

Islamic Influence in Europe

As Islamic armies crossed the Strait of Gibraltar into Spain and Portugal, Europeans saw for themselves the sophistication of Muslim technology. Following the Crusades, or holy wars, Europeans brought back many Islamic luxuries and ideas from the Middle East and western Asia. Islamic influence in Europe was strongest in architecture, medicine, technology, and science. In these areas of knowledge, Muslims scholars led the way. Muslim-controlled cities in Spain, such as Granada and Córdoba, had universities and well-stocked libraries and took on Islamic studies and books. Europeans began translating Islamic works in medicine, astronomy, mathematics, and philosophy. By the 1200s, Islamic knowledge was widespread.

What Europe Got

Islamic advances in **irrigation**—the artificial watering of farmland—allowed more and different types of crops to be grown in Europe. Clocks and **astrolabes** were made in the early period of the Islamic Empire and brought through Spain into Europe. Advances in medicine, such as antiseptics and stitching wounds, also reached Europe. In mathematics, Islamic scholars invented algebra and also gave Europe the **Arabic** number system used today.

Right: Astrolabes were an Islamic invention used by travelers to calculate the position of the stars and planets to help navigation. This elegant astrolabe dates from the late 1000s and possibly came from Spain.

Trade Goods

In Muhammad's lifetime, merchants were held in high regard. Muhammad was a merchant himself. From the earliest days of Islam, trade and commerce were compatible with religion. Markets were situated next to mosques and were open before and after daily prayers. Since everyone came to the mosque to pray, these times of day were good times to do business.

Foreign Trade

The Islamic conquests brought vast areas of the world under a similar culture. Muslim rulers encouraged free trade beyond their borders to Southeast Asia, India, Russia, China, and Europe. Islamic **toleration** of other religions meant

Below: Salt is still traded today in caravans across Africa's deserts. This caravan is carrying salt across the Danakil Desert in Ethiopia in East Africa.

Muslim merchants could do business with Christians, Hindus, Jews, and even **pagans**. Foreign merchants were treated with honor and respect, which also encouraged trade. Islamic rule extended over two important sea trade routes: the Red Sea and the Indian Ocean. It also controlled old overland routes linking Asia and the Mediterranean.

From the late 1000s, Christian and Muslim armies fought wars for control of the Holy Land of Palestine. These wars became known as the Crusades. Many Europeans who traveled to fight in these wars saw the splendors of Islam first hand. The soldiers who went home safely

Trade in Salt

After the Islamic conquest of North Africa, Muslim traders traveled south across the Sahara Desert. They found salt, gold, and slaves. Muslim merchants were not interested in carrying heavy bags of salt all the way back to Arabia and Asia, but salt was a valuable trade item in Africa. A busy trade network developed, taking salt from the salt mines to peoples south of the Sahara. Muslim merchants then traded the salt for gold, slaves, ivory, and cola nuts. They made the long journey across the world's largest desert in caravans.

brought back many wonders from the East: carpets, cloth, spices, glass, ceramics, silk, horses, books, and other luxury items. Rich Europeans were eager to buy such goods, boosting trade between the East and West.

Below: Muslim merchants sell flowers and spices at a market below the Constantine Column in the Ottoman capital of Constantinople (now known as Istanbul).

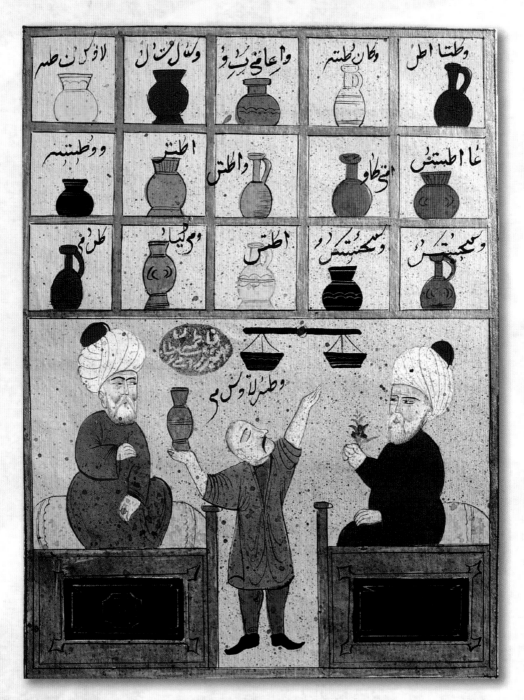

Above: Spices from China, India, and Southeast Asia, such as cinnamon, had healing properties. Here, two Islamic doctors tell a pharmacist how to make some medicines.

Herbs and Spices

Herbs and spices were used in medicine, cooking, and to preserve foods. The trade in spices made more money for Muslim merchants than any other business, except buying and selling slaves. Spices were low in weight but high in value. Even a small bag of spices could be sold at a great profit. Pepper, ginger, cinnamon, cloves, cardamom, mace, myrrh, nutmeg, and musk were among the spices imported from India, China, and Africa. Myrrh was used to make perfumes, medicines, and incense.

Sailing ships followed the Spice Route, a network of sea lanes that stretched more than 7,500 miles (12,070 km) from the Mediterranean to the Far East. The most expensive spices came from a few small islands and coastal regions of Southeast Asia. Muslim merchants risked their lives to sail vast distances to buy and sell the rare spices.

Trading Patterns

The trade goods sold in the Islamic Empire varied over time as fashions and people's tastes changed. New lands were found and new trade partners acquired. Bad weather, piracy, and wars could affect trade and what goods were available to buy and sell. Generally, two types of goods were for sale: cheap local items and costly luxury imports from far away. Merchants handled all types of items, from expensive silk robes to inexpensive sacks of grain. They traded raw materials as well as manufactured goods.

Silks, thread, fabrics, tea, porcelain, rice, spices, and herbs came from China. Cotton, tea, and spices came from India and Southeast Asia, and carpets and cotton from Egypt. Goods from Christian Europe could also be found in Islamic markets: furs, slaves, iron weapons, leather goods, arrows, livestock, and exotic woods. An amazing variety of market goods came from conquered lands. A buyer could choose between birds of prey, plant oils (for cooking, soaps, cosmetics, and burning lamps), dyes such as indigo, swords and daggers, glassware, pottery, leatherwork (such as bags, belts, and saddles), and paintings.

Medical Herbs

Muslim physicians were skilled in health, hygiene, and medicine. They found that many herbs and spices had medicinal uses. *The Canon of Medicine,* written in 1025 by Muslim scholar Ibn Sina, was one of the most important books about using herbs and spices to treat infections and illnesses. It lists more than 800 tested drugs, plants, and minerals, and describes how they should be used. Ibn Sina describes the healing properties of herbs such as senna, sandalwood, rhubarb, myrrh, and rosewater.

Money

Above: These Islamic and Byzantine coins from the 900s were discovered in Britain in 2007. Such finds show how coins were widely exchanged across Europe in Early Islamic times.

In Arabia before Islam, people did not often trade using currency. Instead, they used barter to exchange things, such as gold for spices. As Islamic armies conquered other lands, Muslims came into contact with metal coins and their use as money.

Paper Money

The first people to use bills or paper money were the Chinese. When the Mongols ruled China from the 1200s, their use of paper money amazed the European traveler Marco Polo when he visited the country. Islamic traders also learned of paper money on their visits to China. The danger for trade, however, was printing too much paper money so that it became worthless. Many Muslim traders therefore stuck with gold.

Money and Trust

Coins made of copper, silver, and gold had long been used by the Greeks, Romans, and others. Sums of money were worked out by weighing coins, not by counting them. Coins were often counterfeited, or faked. They were also heavy to carry. For long-distance trade, many merchants used the *suftaja*, or letter of credit. It worked like a traveler's check. Before a merchant set off, he gave his money to a respectable moneychanger, who issued a suftaja for that amount. When the merchant reached his destination, he gave the suftaja to another moneychanger, who paid him for it in coins. The merchant used the coins to buy and sell his goods. Suftajas were so widely accepted that a merchant from Baghdad was sure of payment in China.

Below: This Persian tax collector is busy in the market. Taxes on trade helped to make Muslim states wealthy.

Religious Principles

The **Quran**, the Islamic holy book, gives guidance on religious matters and ritual practice, but also deals with business and social life. Islamic laws on trade and commerce are based on its religious teachings.

One of the main teachings of Islam is that people must deal fairly with one another. Another is that no business dealings by an individual or group should harm others or damage nature. People must answer to God (**Allah**) if they cheat or misuse Earth's resources. So charging interest on a loan (usury) is forbidden in the Quran, since it is not believed to be just. The reason given is that the person making the loan gets money without sharing in the risk of the business venture. That is seen as being unfair to the person borrowing the money.

Luxury Items

Rich people in the Islamic Empire could afford to buy such luxuries as carpets, textiles, jewelry, glassware, cosmetics, furniture, and fine clothing. Some of these luxury goods were made by local workers and were exported to India, China, and Europe. In return, costly spices, ivory, and silks were imported from foreign lands. Many Muslim merchants made their money trading luxury items and the raw materials used to make them.

Precious Metals

Muslim culture frowned on extravagant displays of wealth, so gold and silver were not often used to make household objects or drinking vessels such as cups. Bowls, ornaments, and other items were made from nonmetals, or from cheaper metals such as copper, bronze, or brass.

Below: Carved ivory caskets decorated with fittings of silver and precious stones, such as this one made in Muslim Spain, were rare and expensive trade items highly valued for their beauty.

Muslims valued objects decorated with inlays of enamel, jewels, and glass. Gold and silver were used for coins and fine decoration on objects. Silver was mined in many parts of Asia, but gold had to be brought from west and south Africa. Muslim merchants often used gold in exchange for goods when trading in European markets.

African Ivory

Ivory was an important trade item from Africa to Europe and Asia. Elephant and hippopotamus ivory was traded at Gao, an important Muslim trading city in Mali. In return for the ivory tusks, Muslim merchants traded pottery, glass, and bronze jewelry. Most of the ivory carried north was transported uncut, to later be cut and worked in craftshops. Some ivory, however, was carved into figures and caskets by African craftworkers, and then sold at market or used in exchange trades. Skilled artisans in such cities as Damascus and Baghdad crafted the ivory into intricate carvings to decorate furniture, jewelry, caskets, weapons, and even scientific and medical equipment.

Above: As in the past, Bedouin women from the Arab world today drill holes in gold and silver coins and wear them as a sign of their families' wealth.

Jewelry

The Quran speaks of the beauty of jewelry and gemstones and their place in **Paradise** as wonders of God's creation. Precious stones, such as rubies, emeralds, and pearls, were luxury items that were valuable as trade goods. Making and trading jewelry was supervised by a government inspector to ensure quality. Owning jewelry was a sign of power and social status. Many gems and precious metals from the Islamic world found their way to Europe, often to royal treasuries or churches.

Carpets and Rugs

By the time of the Ottoman Empire (1281–1918), Islamic rugs and carpets had become popular in Europe. The tradition of making carpets, however, had begun much earlier. Muslim worshipers had to prostrate themselves to pray. They did so on small carpets or mats. As Islam spread, so did the making and trading of carpets and rugs. Fine carpets, floor coverings, cushions, and room dividers were traded throughout the Islamic world. The quality of carpets varied. Some were simple rugs made from sheep's wool and goat hair, but others were much more costly carpets woven from fine silk with intricate geometric patterns.

Above: In the Islamic world, carpets, rugs, and blankets were made by hand on simple looms. Threads were dyed in bright colors and woven to create geometric and floral patterns that are still used today.

Luxuries for Ladies

Women in Middle Eastern societies used cosmetics. Ointments scented with musk were particularly highly valued. Cosmetics were made from imported goods such as indigo, saffron, and sandalwood. Women owned ivory combs, metal mirrors, glass vessels to store liquid cosmetics, and decorated pottery jars for ointments. They used make-up applicators carved from ivory.

Below: This piece of fabric from Persia, woven around 1500, shows a youth drinking from a cup and flask. European Crusaders brought fabrics such as this home from the Holy Land. It became the fashion in Europe for wealthy people to wear clothing made from Islamic silks.

Silks and Fine Materials

Until the 1200s, the Chinese had a monopoly on the making of silk from threads spun by certain types of moth caterpillars. Only they knew the secret, which they guarded carefully, and they made enormous profits from selling silk to nobles and royalty around the world.

Silk was also prized by the early Muslim caliphs. In the 1200s, the secret to silk got out to the rest of the world. Silk weaving in the Muslim states exploded. Islamic lands grew rich from silk production and trade. However, as trade in silk grew and it became more common, its value as a symbol of royalty and supreme wealth diminished.

Perfumes and Scents

Scents and spices used to make perfumes were also profitable trade items. Members of the elite classes were fond of scented items. The most expensive perfumes were made from rare natural materials such as musk, ambergris, and camphor from China and the Indian Ocean. Inexpensive scents were made from locally grown flowers.

Scents were used in many items, from perfumes to cosmetics and soaps. People scented their bodies and rooms with perfumes and incense. They added sweet-smelling herbs and spices to food and drink. Certain fragrances were thought to have healing properties. Many medical texts describe how different scents could affect the body and how to use them to treat ailments.

Trading Cities

Before the Islamic Empire, trading cities in Arabia were little more than small towns positioned at key points on trade routes. Mecca, for example, began as a caravan stop between Syria and Yemen. Towns such as Constantinople eventually grew into large trading cities.

Cities in the Desert

As Islam spread, Muslims settled in the towns. They built mosques and markets alongside them. The markets attracted many traders and merchants, who sold and exchanged all types of goods.

The business activity in turn attracted many different craftworkers, teachers, artists, and yet more merchants. These people followed various religions and spoke many languages. In time, the cities became sprawling multicultural cosmopolitan centers.

Islamic cities became focal points for learning, culture, religion, and trade. As merchants and traders traveled farther to buy and sell goods, they took Islam to new places. Merchants also followed the Muslim armies to conquered areas. They built small towns that over time grew into important trade cities. After the Islamic conquest of Spain, for instance, the cities of Córdoba and Seville grew quickly

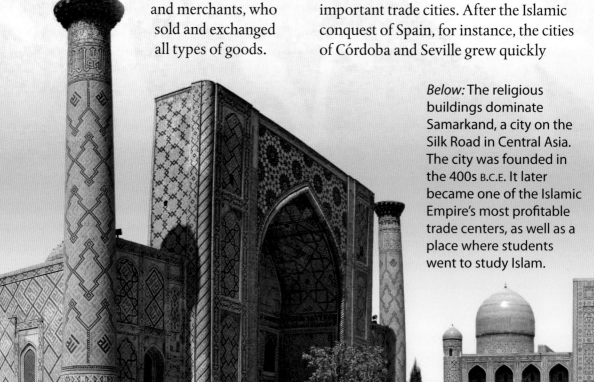

Below: The religious buildings dominate Samarkand, a city on the Silk Road in Central Asia. The city was founded in the 400s B.C.E. It later became one of the Islamic Empire's most profitable trade centers, as well as a place where students went to study Islam.

under Muslim rule to become the most important cities in Spain. Muslim traders and soldiers also settled in China. The Muslim community in Canton became a busy trade center for the Far East.

Above: The once-Christian city of Constantinople became a major center of Islam during the time of the Ottoman Empire. This map of the city dates from the 1500s.

Great Locations

Baghdad, the richest of all Islamic cities, was built as the capital of the Abbasid rulers in the late 700s. It became a hub of international commerce, as many merchants traded in the city's vast markets. Cairo in Egypt became a spice-trading city after the Muslims conquered North Africa. Samarkand, on the Silk Road, became a center for trade and religion. Timbuktu, a city in Mali in West Africa, was on the trade routes for salt, gold, ivory, and slaves. The port city of Aden was a key point for the shipment of gums, resins, and incense.

The Islamic world's economy was based on trade. Rulers taxed trade and wealthy merchants to pay for their governments, armies, and luxuries. Wealthy merchants spent their profits on building hospitals and schools for the community.

Merchant Power

Merchants helped start and develop new trade centers. In return for this service, the rulers gave the merchants respect and protection. As a result, the merchants brought in wealth, and the rulers were seen to be looking after their people. Every big trade city had a market where goods were bought and sold. Port cities had markets in town and along the docks. At a busy port, goods from China, Southeast Asia, India, and from all over the Islamic Empire arrived every day.

The Islamic Empire did not use just one system of weights and measures. Each city and region had its own rules and ways of measuring goods, and these systems changed over time. That makes it difficult for us today to work out how much goods were really worth then.

Left: This gold coin from India around 1650 shows the weighing scales associated with the zodiac or star sign, Libra. The scales would be used to weigh small items.

Standards and Money

"Money" in Islam meant precious metals, such as gold and silver, or commodities or goods such as wheat, barley, dates, and salt. Muslim merchants used two types of coins—the gold *dinar* and the silver *dirham*. A dinar weighed 0.15 ounces (4.25 grams). Its value varied from day to day according to the price of gold. Many Muslim countries today still use these two coins. They also use banknotes with high values of dinar and dirham.

Merchants paid taxes and **tariffs** on trade goods transported on caravans and in ships. The money collected was used by the caliphs for building projects and to pay for their armies. The merchants passed on the extra costs to the buyers in the markets. So a pound of pepper could be less or more expensive, depending on where and when it was sold. The caliphs' inspectors checked weights and measures used in the market. They also set the highest and lowest prices for various goods.

Below: These Turkish merchants are selling fabric, turbans, and other items from their market stalls.

Rural Trade

The gradual spread of agriculture supported the rise of large Islamic cities. A big city needed farmlands and irrigation systems around it to grow food for its increasing population. This growth encouraged people to try new ways of farming and artificially watering the land.

Feeding the People

The most fertile croplands were controlled by a few rich Muslims. They leased, or rented out, their land to farmers, who grew small amounts of crops. This small-scale form of agriculture was common throughout the Islamic Empire, but gradually changed as trading systems improved.

Irrigation Technology

Muslim farmers built on and improved Roman and Persian models for moving water over great distances. These included *qanats* and aqueducts, which are underground and overground water channels. These irrigation systems were used to bring water to lands that had once been dry and barren. Irrigation became common in most agricultural lands, particularly Spain. Crops such as grains, olives, and sugarcane became more profitable as machines to process them—water mills and windmills—were improved.

Below: A modern-day Jordanian herdsman tends his sheep in the desert, just like generations before him.

Merchants introduced new crops from one region to another, including spinach, sugarcane, rice, eggplants, artichokes, oranges, lemons, coconuts, and bananas. These food plants came from the warm, fertile areas of India and Southeast Asia. **Sorghum** was introduced from Africa and cotton from India.

As these new fruits, vegetables, and grains were introduced to Islamic lands, farmers found ways to grow several crops one after the other each year. This made better use of different soils, increased profits, and kept fields fertile. Crops that were once only expensive imports, such as oranges and lemons, were grown by people who had not been able to enjoy

Above: Merchants have been trading livestock since the rise of Islam. Here, modern Arab dealers bargain at a weekly camel market near Aswan in Egypt.

them before. Farmers developed ways to protect soil from erosion, or being worn away. They learned how to modify plants—to improve types of fruit trees, for example—and to control pests.

This agricultural revolution also changed the way people raised animals. Tribes that raised sheep and goats for their own use could raise more animals to be sold at markets, too. Wool and skins were more valued, and this helped develop the leatherworking and textile industries.

Markets and Bazaars

وكاس مجا من عن الحسن حلب   سقسه جها الحب راحته مقتلي

In Islam, religion and trade were closely linked. Nowhere is this better seen than in the markets and bazaars of Muslim cities. Every big city in the Islamic world had a bustling market. Markets were usually in or near the center of town, around the main mosque to which crowds of Muslims came for prayers and community meetings.

Above: In this scene from the 1560s, Persian artisans are busy in the bazaar as shoppers look on. Artisans were skilled workers who set up groups known as guilds to teach their craft and negotiate pay and prices with local rulers.

A Trading Economy

The market was divided according to goods on sale: a silver district, a cloth district, a glass district. Stalls and shops selling luxury goods and religious items were located closest to the mosque. Merchants selling leather, which smelled terrible, were farther away. Big-city markets, like the one in Baghdad, had miles (km) of narrow streets beneath high arched roofs. Small stalls sold food such as sugared almonds and nuts, confections, and dried fruit. They also sold local products such as clothing.

The market district was busy by day but empty at night, when it was patrolled by guards. Markets in smaller towns consisted of one or two narrow streets lined with stalls. Here, merchants sold local merchandise, such as grains and food, but also imports from overseas or other markets.

Courts and Moneychangers

Local rulers usually set the prices of goods to be sold. They set up *quads*, or courts, to listen to disputes and punish anyone caught cheating or stealing. Moneychangers weighed and measured coins. In large cities, they kept sealed bags of coins, ready to pay merchants who came with letters of credit, or *suftaja*,

Right: This modern market is set up near the Great Mosque of Djenné in Mali, Africa —the world's largest mud-brick structure.

from other cities. Rural markets were more informal, with people often gathering outside town. Farmers and craftspeople met to trade food and livestock, and to exchange, buy, and sell locally made goods.

Market Inspectors

To keep merchants honest, most cities employed *muhtasib*, or market inspectors. The inspectors made sure that weighing scales and measuring rules were accurate. They also made sure that merchants and shoppers kept to Islamic rules of cleanliness, public order, and morality. The inspectors watched for tricks used by dishonest merchants to cheat their customers. Such tricks included blowing gently on balance scales to make them drop, or sticking wax underneath the scales to add weight.

The Slave Trade

The slave trade was an important part of the Islamic economy. Slaves had been bought and sold from before the first Muslim conquests in the 600s. The trade continued until it was abolished by the Ottoman Empire in the early 1900s. Slaves provided most of the labor force in the cities and on farms. Slave-soldiers made up the largest part of most Islamic armies.

Slaves in the Market

Slaves were people who were owned, and made to work for little or no pay. A few slaves worked as field hands on farms. Most slaves were skilled workers in the towns and cities. Slave markets were always full of newly arrived captives. These people included Christians sold by Venetian traders; soldiers taken as prisoners of war; and Africans sold to Arab slave traders, often by their own tribes.

Below: Muslim slave traders in Africa usually bought slaves from peaceful, slave-trading tribes, with whom the traders had friendly links.

Most slaves were slaves from birth, since the children of a slave automatically became slaves themselves. The only exception to this rule was when a slave's owner, or master, was the father of the slave's child. By Islamic law, no person could be the slave of his father. Such a child would be free, even though its mother remained a slave.

Above: Although this drawing of an Egyptian slave market from about 1800 shows Black slaves, most slaves sold in bazaars were light-skinned and came from areas that had been conquered by Muslim armies.

Slaves were regarded as luxury goods. Slave merchants usually had their own markets or, in larger cities, their own section of the bazaar. Depending on their age, health, and gender, one slave could be worth thousands of dinars. Generally, white slaves cost more than slaves with darker skin, and women—especially if they were young, beautiful, and well-educated—were highly prized.

Slaves were also valued according to the jobs they could do. Female slaves worked as servants, nursemaids, and concubines (sex slaves). Male slaves might become bodyguards or work as butchers, dyers, tailors, artisans, and accountants.

Slave Soldiers

Some male slaves were trained to fight in the Islamic armies. Christian boys, often brought from Eastern Europe or Russia, were trained to fight for a rich master or a ruler. They could rise in rank through good deeds. One group of slave-soldiers, known as the Mamluks, became very powerful. They overthrew the Egyptian sultans in the 1200s and ruled Egypt for 256 years.

Trade by Land and Sea

Trade routes connected Muslim societies to those around them. The Incense Trail linked India, Oman, and Yemen to Mediterranean ports. The Silk Road stretched from China to the Mediterranean Sea. Traveling along these routes in either direction was risky.

Safely in Numbers

Trade caravans faced danger from thieves, harsh weather, sandstorms, mountains, and deserts. Merchants sometimes took along their family and servants. They hired local guides and translators, so they could talk with strangers they met. They also took along camel drivers, doctors

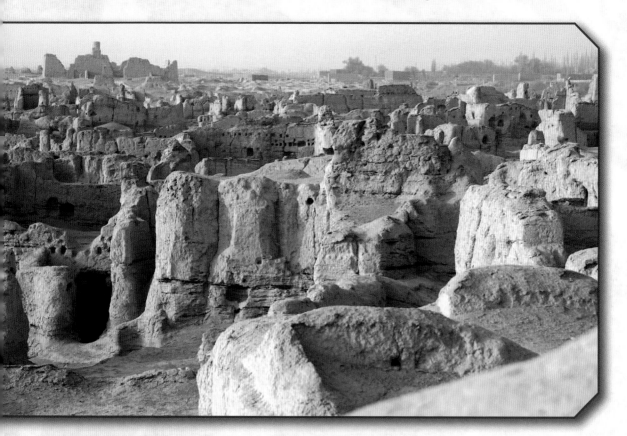

Above: During the 700s and 800s, a permanent camp of 6,000 armed men were stationed in this now-ruined city of Jiaohe in China to guard caravans on the Silk Road.

and vets, cooks, and armed guards. Other travelers, such as monks and religious teachers, entertainers, adventurers, even criminals and escaped slaves, would join the larger caravans of merchants. Traveling in a caravan offered protection, as well as company on the long journey.

A Long Journey

A trip could last for weeks, since a caravan could travel only about 12 to 18 miles (19 to 29 km) a day. Carried on camels, horses, or other animals, trade goods had to be small and light but also valuable. They included silks, precious stones, spices, herbs, ivory, amber, and ceramics. Caravans traveling east often carried incense, glass, dates, and sugared dried fruits, which were considered an exotic delicacy in China. Perishable foods, such as watermelon and honeydew melons, were packed in lead containers filled with snow to keep them fresh.

Caravans did not often make the full journey. Goods were usually moved in stages. They were bought and sold in cities along the route. New merchants then carried them farther. Along the way were stopping places, called *caravanserai*. These were about a day's journey apart. They had a water source and were defended against attack. These rest stops allowed caravan travelers to eat, sleep, and look after their animals. People traveling in a caravan could stay at a caravanserai for free, only paying for their food.

Desert Demons

Ibn Battuta (1304–1369) was an Islamic traveler who spent almost 30 years journeying throughout the world. On his travels, he joined a caravan across North Africa. He described crossing the Sahara Desert: "That desert is haunted by demons . . . For there is no visible road or track in these parts, nothing but sand blown hither and thither by the wind. You see hills of sand in one place, and afterward you will see them moved to quite another place."

Right: Small but expensive items, such as these spices and herbs, were carried across Asia along the Silk Road.

Trade By Sea

From the time of Muhammad, sea trade was vital to the Islamic Empire. In the Quran, merchant ships are mentioned as a sign of God's reward: "He sends winds as tokens of glad tidings . . . that ships may sail by His command so you may seek His bounty and be grateful." The sea routes to the East and China were just as dangerous as the overland routes because of pirates and storms. However, a ship could carry more goods at less expense than a land caravan.

Trade ports grew into busy cities. Here, ships filled with goods from the East were unloaded. The goods were repacked onto caravans and sent west. Muslim shipping merchants had been trading porcelain, spices, and gold with Europeans since the 1200s. By the 1400s, the Italian city-states of Venice, Genoa, and Naples had become powerful through trade. They were trading products with Islamic merchants and selling them to the rest of Europe, making enormous profits and growing rich in the process.

Trade Rivals and War

The Portuguese were the first Europeans to discover a route to the East by sea. In the late 1400s, they sent sailing ships around the southern tip of Africa across the Indian Ocean to India. For the first time, Asian merchants faced a real threat to their trade networks and new competition in their spice trade. At the same time, trade throughout Muslim lands was starting to decline. The Portuguese had a clear goal—to invade the Islamic Empire and control the Muslim trade routes.

Below: The decoration of these merchant homes in Venice, Italy, was influenced by Islamic design. Venetian merchants had links to the spice trade.

Dhows

Arab merchants crossed the Indian Ocean in seagoing ships called *dhows*. Dhows were long, wooden sailing vessels with lateen (triangular) sails. They were built by tying wooden planks together with ropes. Dhows could carry heavy trade goods such as fruits, timber, and livestock, as well as fresh water.

Below: Spanish trading ships, with soldiers and Moors onboard, tried to dominate the sea routes from Europe to Asia.

Trade in Decline

From the 1400s, the Islamic world was dominated by the Ottoman Empire. The Ottoman sultans, with their capital in Constantinople, saw trade as a way to make money for their empire. Then European sea traders began to take over the Mediterranean sea routes and challenge Muslim traders in the Indian Ocean. They wanted to control the trade in spices, gold, slaves, and other goods.

Below: Venice and the Ottoman Empire often fought for control of the Mediterranean Sea. Here the Venetian ambassador (seated, in black) visits the Ottoman royal court for peace talks.

Europe and the New World

At this time, Europe was undergoing an intellectual awakening, or rebirth, known as the Renaissance. This resulted in advances in weapons, shipbuilding, and navigation. Europeans had new weapons, such as handguns and cannons, and better ships. They were now better able to challenge established trade networks in the Mediterranean and the Indian Ocean.

The Ottomans Fight Back

In 1538, the Portuguese threatened to capture the town of Aden in Yemen. This trade port was in a key location, at entrance to the Red Sea. The Ottomans sent a huge fleet of ships and soldiers to defend the city. They captured several Portuguese ships and stopped the Europeans from taking control.

This battle began a long conflict between the Ottomans and the Portuguese. For more than 25 years, the two battled for control of trade routes and trade cities in the Indian Ocean. Neither side gained an advantage. Finally, the Portuguese turned their attention to controlling the sea route to Asia around the tip of South Africa.

A New World Order

Gradually, Europeans gained more economic power in the world. They also discovered the Americas and opened up new trading markets to the West. The Ottomans were outmaneuvered and outgunned. They lost control of ocean trade westward from India and Southeast Asia.

As their trade weakened, so did the Ottoman Empire. By the 1800s, the Industrial Revolution in Europe meant that inexpensive factory-made goods were flooding into Islamic markets, displacing handcrafted luxury items. Islamic trade networks survived only on a small scale, between local markets. International trade was now run by new world powers.

Battle of Lepanto

In October 1571, a large European naval force of more than 200 ships filled with soldiers went into battle with an equally strong Ottoman fleet. The battle of Lepanto was fought off the coast of Greece. After a four-hour battle, the Europeans won, taking thousands of men captive. The Ottoman commander, Ali Pasha, was captured and beheaded. The victory boosted European military and trading confidence against the Ottomans.

Above: European explorer Christopher Columbus reached the Americas by ship in 1492. With a few years, many trade networks had shifted from Asia to the Americas.

Biographies

Here are short biographies of some of the most important and famous Muslim traders, merchants, and explorers of the early Islamic world. Their influence and impact on trade and the spread of Islam helped establish and maintain Muslim culture over large areas of the world for hundreds of years.

The Prophet Muhammad

Muhammad was born into an Arabian merchant family in 570. As a young man, he made several trade expeditions between Mecca and Palestine. He experienced religious revelations that he said were messages from God. These were recorded in the holy book, the *Quran*, and he founded the religion of Islam. By the time of his death in 632, Islam had become the main religion of Arabia.

Tamim Ibn Bahr

The Arab traveler Tamim Ibn Bahr visited Karabalghasun in the Uighur Empire of western China in about 821. It is likely Ibn Bahr was sent on his long trip for political reasons. He wrote of his surprise and admiration in seeing a thriving town in a rich country. The popular idea among Muslims at this time was that only wild nomads lived in this remote area.

Ibn Abd Al-Hakam

One of the earliest surviving histories of the Islamic conquest of Spain is al-Hakam's *The History of the Conquest of Egypt and North Africa and Spain*. Al-Hakam died around 870, and although his book was written 150 to 200 years after the events it describes, Islamic historians often relied on it for information.

Ahmad Ibn Fadlan

In 921, the Caliph of Baghdad sent Ibn Fadlan on a government mission to the king of the Bulgars. Ibn Fadlan wrote an account of his trip, during which he met Rus, or Viking, traders from Scandinavia.

Naser-E Khosraw

Naser-e Khosraw was born in 1003 in Persia. He gave up his job and set out to see the world at age 42. He joined a caravan across Persia into Syria, writing about his adventures and the peoples he met in a book called the *Safarnama*.

Usamah Ibn Munqidh

Ibn Munqidh was a Muslim diplomat from Syria who fought against the Crusaders in the 1100s. Although the Christian soldiers were his rivals, he made friends with many of them. His writings describe his wartime experiences.

Above: Suleiman, known to Europeans as the Magnificent and to the Ottomans as the Lawgiver, was one of the most powerful and talented sultans.

Ma Huan

Ma Huan accompanied the famous Chinese admiral Zheng He on three Silk Road expeditions. A Chinese Muslim, Ma Huan's knowledge of Arabic and other languages made him a useful translator. He made detailed notes about the places he visited, writing them all down in 1431.

Zahiruddin Muhammad Babur

Born in 1483, Babur was a Muslim warrior and descendant of the great conqueror Genghis Khan, who founded the Mongol Empire in Central Asia. What is known of Babur's life comes mainly from his autobiography, the *Baburnama*. In this book, he describes his early life in Central Asia and how he led an army into northern India and founded the Mughal Empire. Babur was an educated Muslim and his book is filled with observations of the world. He writes about his political and military struggles, and also gives descriptions of plants and animals, architecture, music, and literature. Most historians consider his to be the only true autobiography in Islamic literature.

Ibn Battuta

Considered one of the greatest travelers of all time, Ibn Battuta covered some 75,000 miles (120,700 km) during his lifetime. Ibn Battuta was born in 1304 in Tangier in North Africa. In his twenties, he discovered a love for travel, and spent most of his adult life traveling through the Islamic Empire. He visited North and West Africa, Europe, India, Central and Southeast Asia, and China. He published an extensive account of his travels, the *Rihla*, in 1355.

Suleiman the Magnificent

Sultan of the Ottoman Empire from 1520 to 1566, he boosted Islamic trade and commerce to its highest levels. Under his rule, the Ottoman fleet controlled sea trade throughout the Persian Gulf and the Mediterranean and Red seas.

The Spread of Islamic Trade and Influence

The Islamic Empire and its trade had a huge impact on the rest of the world. Muslim merchants journeyed throughout the known world of Europe, Africa, and Asia, spreading the Muslim faith as they did so. They also took with them Islam's knowledge of botany, agriculture, medicine, mathematics, astronomy, commerce, and many other sciences and arts.

The cities that the Muslim armies conquered became centers of international trade, learning, and culture. People of all religions were not only tolerated but welcomed in the Islamic Empire. Islamic scholars preserved much Ancient Roman and Greek knowledge and thought, long before Europe rediscovered this important ancient learning during the 1400s.

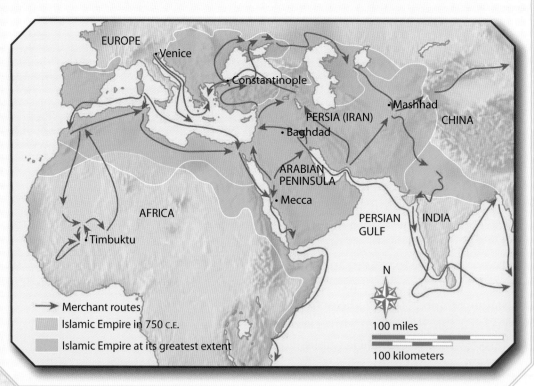

EUROPE
Venice
Constantinople
Mashhad
PERSIA (IRAN)
CHINA
Baghdad
ARABIAN PENINSULA
Mecca
AFRICA
PERSIAN GULF
INDIA
Timbuktu
N

→ Merchant routes
Islamic Empire in 750 C.E.
Islamic Empire at its greatest extent

100 miles
100 kilometers

Islamic World

570 Birth of Muhammad

610 Muhammad receives the first of his revelations from God, the messages that become Islam

630 Conquest of Mecca

632 Muhammad dies

633–750 Islamic caliphs and leaders invade and conquer most of the Arab world, creating the Islamic Empire

754 Baghdad becomes the capital of the Islamic Empire

800s Written collections of the *Hadiths* (sayings of the Prophet) are compiled

821 Tamim Ibn Bahr visits Uighur Empire of western China

1045 Naser-e Khosraw sets out to travel the Islamic world

1099 Christian Crusaders capture Jerusalem

1221 Genghis Khan and the Mongols enter Persia and devastate Islamic Empire until the Mongols are defeated in Egypt in 1260

1281 Ottoman Empire begins

1325 Ibn Battuta begins his lifelong travels

1453 Ottomans take Constantinople

1492 Europeans reconquer Spain and drive out the Muslims

1526 Babur conquers India and sets up Mughal Empire

1571 Battle of Lepanto between the Ottomans and Europeans ends the Islamic control over Mediterranean Sea trade

Rest of the World

950s Latin manuscript in Spain introduces Islamic astrolabe and astronomy to Europe

1075–1098 Earliest known Western medical text written by a Muslim and published in Italy

1202 Italian mathematician Fibonacci persuades Europeans to adopt the Arabic number system

1271 Italian Marco Polo travels through Islamic Empire to China

1405 Chinese admiral Zheng He begins first of seven voyages around South East Asia and the Indian Ocean

1427 Portuguese sailors begin to explore coast of Africa and seek new sea route to India

1455 Europe's first printed book, the *Gutenberg Bible*, is completed

1485–1516 Leonardo da Vinci makes accurate anatomical drawings

1494 Italian Luca Pacioli's important mathematics text, including algebra, is written

1498 Portuguese sailor Vasco da Gama sails round Africa to India

1500s Portuguese dominate trade in the Indian Ocean

1507 Portuguese seize Hormuz at mouth of Persian Gulf

1519 Magellan sets out to circumnavigate the globe by sea

1538 Ottomans and Portuguese fight for control of Aden

1564 Copernicus suggests the planets orbit the Sun, not Earth

Glossary

agriculture The commerce of farming

Allah The one true God of Islam; from *al* (the) *ilah* (god)

Arabic The language of Arabia; something or someone of or from Arabia

Arab A person from Arabia

astrolabe A navigation instrument that relies on the position of stars in the sky

barter Trade involving the exchange of goods; it does not require money

bazaar Large area where merchants buy and sell goods

caliphate An Islamic state ruled by caliphs, Muhammad's successors

caravans Groups of people and animals traveling together, usually transporting trade goods

commerce Everything related to trade, including banking and transportation

Crusades Series of religious wars fought between European Christians and Muslims in Palestine, Egypt, and Turkey

empire A large area made up of different societies ruled by one leader

irrigation The artificial watering of crops often involving pumps and ditches

Islam The religion or faith based on God's messages to Muhammad

Mecca The holiest city of Islam, in the west of Arabia

merchants Buyers and sellers of goods

moneychangers People who exchange one currency for another

Moors A European term for North African Muslims

mosques Buildings used as Muslim places of worship or houses of prayer

Muslim A person who follows the faith of Islam

nomads People with no fixed home, who instead move from place to place

pagans People who follow a religion with many gods or idols

Paradise Heaven; life after death

peninsula An area of land projecting from the mainland into a sea or lake

porcelain Pottery made from very fine clay

prophet A religious teacher who was inspired by God, as Muhammad was

Quran Islam's holy book, containing the messages Muhammad said came from God

sorghum A grass that produces grain to make flour and bread

suftaja A letter of credit

sultan A Muslim king or ruler

tariffs Taxes charged by the government on imported goods

toleration Letting other people think, believe, or act as they wish

trade The business of goods passing from person to person involving barter or buying and selling

Further Information

Books

Barnard, Bryn. *The Genius of Islam: How Muslims Made the Modern World.* New York: Knopf Books For Young Readers, 2011.

Davis, Lucile. *Life During the Great Civilizations: The Ottoman Empire.* San Diego: Blackbirch Press, 2004.

Hinds, Kathryn. *The City* (Life in the Medieval Muslim World). New York: Marshall Cavendish, 2008.

Rumford, James. *Traveling Man: The Journey of Ibn Battuta, 1325–1354.* New York: Houghton Mifflin, 2001.

Spilsbury, Louise and Richard. *The Islamic Empires* (Time Travel Guides). Bloomington: Raintree, 2007.

Websites

Medieval Islamic Economy
www.historyforkids.org/learn/islam/economy

India—The Roaring Trade Partner of Yore
www.gatewayforindia.com/articles/tradeyore.htm

Middle Ages Trade & Commerce
www.middle-ages.org.uk/middle-ages-trade-commerce.htm

The Silk Road: Linking Europe and Asia Through Trade
http://library.thinkquest.org/13406/sr

History of the Indian Ocean
www.indianoceanhistory.org

Index